ENJOYING KINGDOM PROSPERITY: SECRET ACCESS TO KINGDOM PROSPERITY

ENGR. SAMUEL CHUKWUBUIDE STEPHEN

DEDICATION

**THIS BOOK IS DEDICATED TO ALMIGHTY GOD WHO GIVES
INSPIRATION TO MANKIND.**

CONTENTS

ACKNOWLEDGMENTS

MY THANKS GO TO ALMIGHTY GOD FOR HIS INFINITE MERCIES AND   ABUNDANCE GRACES TO HUMANITY.
MY SINCERE GRATITUDE GOES TO MY PARENTS DEACON STEPHEN EDEH AND LATE MRS. PATRICIA EDEH.
MY SPECIAL THANKS ALSO GO TO MY PRINTER PILLAR WEALTH GLOBAL COMMUNICATION RESOURCES WHO FROM INCEPTION OF THIS BOOK SEE THAT IT COMES TO REALITY. AND I ALSO TAKE RESPONSIBILITY SHOULD THERE BE ANY ERROR IN THIS EDITION AND PROMISE TO IMPROVE ON IT IN THE NEXT EDITION.   FINALLY, I EXPRESS MY GRATITUDE AND LOVE TO MY SIBLINGS, EVERY MEMBER OF MY FAMILY FOR THEIR UNDERSTANDING AND SUPPORT IN MAKING THIS BOOK A REALITY.

1 CHAPTER ONE
SECRET: ACCESS TO KINDOM PROSPERITY.

IN THE KINGDOM OF GOD, WE TRIUMPH WITH WHAT IS CALLED SECRET(IDEAS). ONE SECRET REVIEW TO YOU BY GOD CAN TAKE YOU TO THE TOP.   THE ENTIRE WORLD, ECONOMIC, BUSINESS AND SCIENTIFIC WORLD HAS ONE SECRET TO ANOTHER.   NO MORTAL MAN WILL TELL YOU SECRET OF THEIR PROSPERITY.
       PROSPERITY IS A STATE OF ALL-ROUND SUCCESS AND WELLBEING.

Always ask God to review to you the secret of what to do to achieve success.
                           One secret from the Holy Spirit can establish you.   Prosperity begins with idea; prosperity is not all about money.   Money does not bring idea but ideas bring money.   Shift your focus on job, appointment, and focus on divine secret and you will be a star.
Ask God to show you Divine secret, wealth is a function of revealed secret from God.   Prosperity is not only money; prosperity is a round success.
       Psalm 25:4(KJV)-Show me your ways, O LORD; teach me your path.   One thing about prosperity is secret, once secret is review to you, you will make a star.
              SCRIPTURAL EXAMPLE OF THOSE THAT PROSPER:

1.Abraham and Isaac:

Genesis 26:14(KJV)-For he had possessions of flocks and possessions of herds and a great number of servants. So, the philistines envied him.

2. Jacob and joseph:

Genesis41:4-Then it came to pass, at the end of two full years, that pharaoh had a dream; and behold, he stood by the river.

Job29:4(KJV)-just as I was in the days of my prime, when the friendly counsel of God was over my tent;

3.Job: Job1:3(KJV)-Also, his possessions were seven thousand sheep, three thousand camels, five hundred yoke of oxen, five hundred female donkeys, and a very large house hold, so that this man was the greatest of all the people of the East.

4.Daniel.

Daniel2:30,47-49(KJV)-"But as for me, this secret has not been revealed to me because I have more wisdom than anyone living, but for our sakes who make known the interpretation to the king, and that you may know the thoughts of your heart.47-The king answered Daniel, and said, "Truly your God is the God of gods, the Lord of kings, and a revealed of secrets, since you could reveal this secret. 48-Then the king promoted Daniel and gave him many great gifts; and he made him ruler over the whole province of Babylon, and chief administrator over all the wise men of the Babylon.49-Also Daniel petitioned the king, and he set Shadrach, Meshach and Abed-Nego over the affairs of the province of Babylon; but Daniel sat in the gate of the king.

5. Paul: Galatians 2:2   (KJV)-And I went up by revelation, and communicated to them that Gospel which I preach among the Gentiles, but privately to those who were of reputation, lest by any means I might run, or had run, in vain.

HOW TO ENCOUNTER SECRET FOR PROSPRITY: 1. Pray to God and specifically ask for secret.

Jeremiah33:3(KJV)- 'Call to Me, and I will answer you, and show you great and mighty things, which you do not know.

2.Pray in Holy Spirit

Philemon 1:14(KJV)-But without your consent I wanted to do nothing, that your good deed might not be by compulsion, as it were, but voluntary.

1 Corinthians 2:10-12(KJV)-But God has revealed them to us through His spirit. For the Spirit searches all things, yes, the deep things of God.   11-For what man knows the things of a man except the spirit of the man which is in him? Even so no one knows the things of God except the Spirit of God.

12-Now we have received, not the Spirit of the world, but the Spirit who is from God, that we might know the things that have been freely given to us by God.

3.Gives sacrificially offering: Abraham did not know there was a ram until he gave sacrificial offering.

Genesis22:13(KJV)-Then Abraham; lifted his eyes and looked, and there behind him was a ram caught in a thicket by its horns. So, Abraham went and took the ram, and offered it up for burnt offering instead of his son.

When you give sacrificially God will review to you secret.

1corinthians 2:9(KJV)-But as it is written: "Eye has not seen, nor ear heard, nor have entered into the heart of a man the things God has prepared for those who love Him."
4.Be sensitive to leading of Holy Spirit per time.

Revelation1:10(KJV)-I was in the Spirit on the Lord's Day, and I heard behind me a loud voice, as of a trumpet,
5. Learn to worship God.
In worship you attract God attention.
Isaiah 30:29-31(KJV)-You shall have a song as in the night when a holy festival is kept, and gladness of heart as when one goes with a flute, to come into the mountain of the LORD, to the Mighty one of Israel.30- The LORD will cause His glorious voice to be heard, and show the descent of His arm, with the indignation of His anger and the flame of a devouring fire, with scattering, tempest, and hailstones.31-For through the voice of the LORD Assyria will be beaten down, who struck with a rod.

6.Through God's word.
Learn to be intelligent and study God's word.

Psalm119:105(KJV)-Your word is a lamp to my feet and a light to my path.

Proverb22:29(KJV)-Do you see a man who excels in his work? He will stand before kings; he will not stand before unknown men.

2.CHAPTER TWO

PATHWAY TO KINGDOM PROSPERITY

PROSPERITY IS A CENTER OF GOD VISION AND WISDOM.

PEOPLE ARE FRUSTRATED ON EARTH BECAUSE THEY ARE NOT WHERE GOD WANT THEM TO BE.

JOEL2:7-8(KJV)-THEY RUN LIKE MIGHTY MEN, THEY CLIMB THE WALL LIKE MEN OF WAR; EVERY ONE MARCHES IN FORMATION, AND THEY DO NOT BREAK RANKS. 8-THEY DO NOT PUSH ONE ANOTHER; EVERY ONE MARCHES IN HIS OWN COLUMN. AND WHEN THEY LUNGE BETWEEN THE WEAPONS, THEY ARE NOT CUT DOWN.

PROSPERITY IS TO BE ALL-ROUND WELLBEING. YOU CANNOT

BOOK TITLE

BE LIKE SOMEONE ELSE IF YOU WANT TO BE PROSPERED.

TO PROSPER, YOU MUST EMBRACE YOUR INDIVIDUALITY IN CHRIST HAVING.

HOW TO PROSPER IN LIFE:

1.Discover your purpose.
Isaiah 46:10(KJV)-Declaring the end from the beginning, and from ancient times things that are not yet done, saying, 'My counsel shall stand, and I will do all My pleasure,'
Before you were born God have planned what you will be.

Jeremiah1:15(KJV)- "Before I formed you in the womb, I knew you; before you were born, I sanctified you; and I ordained you a prophet to the nations."

There are many things you want to do but you will not prosper until you discover what God want you to be on earth.

God have already ordained a purpose for us, so to prosper as believers, we must discover it.
Galatians 1:15(KJV)-But when its pleased God, who separated me from my mother's womb and called me through His grace,

your prosperity is not according to your preference, but what God want you to do.

Proverb 19:21(KJV)-There are many plans in a man's heart, Nevertheless the Lord's counsel--that will stand.

Your purpose is not your decision, it is your responsibility to discover it.
Even identical twins don't have the same finger print.

Your prosperity is tied to your discovery of the problem you were maid to discover.
1 corinthians2:9,16(KJV)-But "Eye has not seen, nor ear heard, nor have entered into the heart of a man the things which God has prepared for those who love Him." 16-For "Who has known the mind of the Lord that he may instruct Him?" But we have the mind of Christ.

1corinthian 12:11,24(KJV)-But one and the same Spirit works all these things, distributing to each one individual as He wills. 24-but our presentable parts have no need. but God composed the body, having given greater honor to that part which lacks it,

matthew25:15(KJV)- "And to one he gave five talents, to another two, and to another one, to each according to his own ability;

and immediately he went on a journey.

Everyone has a God-given gift, there is no ungifted person.

The day you will discover your purpose on earth you will grow abundantly.

Your prosperity cannot begin until you discover purpose.

2.Have a sense of commitment to your assignment.

some of us have discovered their purpose, but why are we not prospering?

Commitment is the willingness to employ the required forces towards a set goal; it can be defined as intelligent work.

Proverb13:4(KJV)-the soul of a sluggard desires, and has nothing: but the soul of intelligent shall be made rich.

Commitment is also the willingness to employ all the skill to prosper.

John5:17(KJV)-But Jesus answered them, "My Father has been working until now, and I have been working."

John 9:4(KJV)- "I must work the works of Him who sent Me while it is day; the night is coming when no one can work.

Lack of commitment can turn a man with prosperous work to be destitute.

You must have a sense of duty to make progress.

Proverb22:29(KJV)-Do you see a man who excels in his work? He will stand before the kings; he will not stand before unknown men.

The top is for diligent while the slothful remains at bottom.

Proverb12:24(KJV)-The hand of the diligent will rules, but the slothful will be put to forced labor.

Going to work does not means you are working; it is your productivity that show you are working.

Always ask yourself what you have achieve.

Psalm1:3(KJV)-He shall be like a tree planted by rivers of water, that brings forth its fruit in its season, whose leaf also shall not wither; And whatever he does shall prosper.

Stop looking for cheap and free money that will not last.

Giving without working is wasting your seed because there is no part of contact for God to bless you.

Any money that does not gotten by labor will vanish.

Proverb13:11(KJV)-Wealth gained by Dishonesty will be diminished, but he who gathers by labor will increase.

Your prosperity is tied and linked to your commitment to duty.

Go and work, if there is no work you create one.

1 Samuel2:9(KJV)-He will guard the feet of His saints, but the wicked shall be silent in darkness. "for by strength no man shall prevail.

3. Sow Consistently.

you should sow continuously to prosper, inconsistently will hinder your progress.

Galatians 6:9(KJV)-And let us grow weary while doing good, for in due season we shall reap if we do not lose heart.

If you don't want things to be tight to you pay your tithe.

Malachi 3:8-11(KJV)- "Will a man rob God? Yet you have robbed Me! But you say, 'In what way have we robbed You?' In tithes and offerings.9- You are cursed with a curse, for you have robbed Me, even this whole nation. 10-Bring all the tithes into the storehouse, that there may be food in My house, and prove Me now in this," says the LORD of hosts, if I will not open for you the windows of heaven And pour out for you such blessing That there will not be room enough to receive it. 11- "And I will rebuke the devourer for your sakes, so that he will not destroy the fruit of your ground, nor shall the vine fail to bear fruit for you in the field," says the LORD of hosts;

Genesis8:22(KJV)-"While the earth remains, seedtime and harvest, and cold and heat, and winter and summer and day and night shall not cease."

Lack of faith and doubt in the character of God are the main reason believers do not give tithe.

Numbers23:10(KJV)-Who can count the dust of Jacob, or number one-fourth of Israel? Let me die the death of the righteous, and let my end be like his!"

Luke6:38(KJV)- "Give, and it will be given to you: good measure, pressed down, shaken together, and running over will be put into your bosom. For with the same measure that you use, it will be measured back to you."

Proverb 11:24-25(KJV)-There is one who scatters; yet increases more; and there is one who withholds more than is right, but it leads to poverty. 25-The generous soul will be made rich, and he will also be watered himself.

Faithlessness and doubting the character of God are the main Reason people do not give.

Proverb11:4(KJV)-Riches do not profit in the day of wrath, but righteousness delivers from death.

BOOK TITLE

No collector can prosper be a giver, be free hand. The size of your seed determines the harvest you will get.
Discover your purpose in life, never lost your place in life. You give to be comfortable not offline.

3. CHAPTER THREE

DISCIPLINE PATHWAY TO KINGDOM PROSPERITY

Discipline path-way to kingdom prosperity.
It is those who are disciplined by the word standard not world standard will not regret on earth.

To be lawless is to be lifeless, life is a race and we must all run to win.
1 Corinthians9:24-27(KJV)-Do you not know that those who run in a race all run, but one receives the prize? Run in such a way that you may obtain it. 25-And everyone who competes for the prize is temperate in all things. Now they do it to obtain a perishable crown, but we for an imperishable crown. 26-Therefore I run thus: not with uncertainty. Thus I fight: not as one who beats the air. 27-But I discipline my body and bring it into subjection, lest, when I have preached to others, I myself should become disqualified. Discipline is the ability to make yourself to do what you should do, when you can do it whether you feel like or not.
Discipline is mandatory if you want to prosper, you must have a discipline if you want to prosper.

Excuses is an enemy of discipline, no one is focus, prosperous or Dedicated until he or she is Discipline.

The main reason for financial problem in life is lack of discipline; if you lack discipline, you have lost a great thing in life (Matthew25:14-28).

You cannot live as you like and expect instant testimony, it is what you do with what you have today that determines your prosperity. You can only increase when you have use what you have now.
Discipline is a sign of maturity; maturity is demand with delay of ratification.

Ecclesiastes10:16-18(CEV)-A country is in for trouble when its ruler is childish, and its leaders party all day long. 17-But a nation will prosper when its ruler is mature, and its leaders don't party too much. 18-some people are too lazy to fix a leaky roof—then the house fall in. Don't bring the pleasures of tomorrow into today by putting yourself under pleasure.

Discipline is what is right not what you like, stop eating your tomorrow because of indiscipline, don't bring the pleasures of tomorrow into today and regret it tomorrow.

Nothing work without you working, you cannot be going to work late and expect to be prosperous.

Discipline is simply meaning self- control; Self-discipline is putting yourself under a law of necessity, self-discipline is operating in self-control, self-discipline also means you can control yourself.

For you to be known, you must say No to any habit that want to destroy you, Discipline is mandatory if you want to prosper.

Psalm65:2(CEV)-Everyone will come to you because you answer prayer.

1Corinthians 9:27(KJV)-I keep my body under control and make it my slave, so I won't lose out after telling the good news to others.

Discipline is controller of Destiny. Discipline is the capacity to restrain desires and Delay gratification.

1Corinthians 6:12(CEV)-Some of you says, "We can do anything we want to." But I tell you that not everything is good for us. So, I refuse to let anything have power over me.

4 CHAPTER FOUR

AREAS TO DISCIPLINE YOURSELF TO ENJOY KINGDOM PROSPERITY

1. SPENDING: Avoid frivolous spending of the money at your disposal.

Learn to spend your money according to your budget, never spend more than you earn.

Proverb21:20(CEV)-Be sensible and store up precious treasures-don't waste them like a fool.

2.LIFESTYLES: Avoid excessive visiting, Habitual excessive visiting will lead to poverty.

Proverb 23:2,19-21(KJV)-Don't go and stuff yourself! That would be just the same as cutting your throat. 19-Listen to me, my children! Be wise and have enough sense to follow the right path. 20-Don't be a heavy drinker or stuff yourself with food. 21-it will make feel drowsy, and you will end up poor with only rag to wear.

Avoid excessive feasting, Do a weeding and other occasions according to size. Don't borrow to do wedding or party, Stop the lifestyle of wasting millions of monies.

1Timothy 6:8(KJV)-And having food and clothing, with these we shall be content.

3.SLEEP: Too much sleep will make you a flipper.

No wealthy man on earth sleep off, your sleep should be to rest not to habit.

Proverb6:10-11(KJV)-A little sleep, a little slumber, a little folding of the Hands to sleep—11-so shall your poverty come on you like a robber, and you're like an armed man.

There is no wealthy man that is not an early riser, even medical   doctors don't sleep during exam.

4.INCOME: Discipline yourself by living below your income, never spend more than you earn.

Luke 14:28-29(KJV)- "For which of you, intending to build a tower, does not sit down first and count the cost, whether he has enough to finish it—29-"lest, after he has laid the foundation, and is not able to finish it, all who see it begin to mock him,

To avoid mockery and poverty don't live above your income, Don't live and   put your hope to another man money.

The best way to live financially buoyancy is not living below your means but increasing your means and income.

stop planning your life with another man's wealth, stop the life styles of borrowing money.

Learn to spend your income to avoid mockery and poverty.

Deuteronomy 28:12(KJV)- "The LORD will open to you His good treasure, the heavens, to give the rain to your land in its season, and bless all the work of your hand. You shall lend to many nations, but you shall not borrow.

Borrowing is Emptying your future ahead of present.
Proverb 22:7(KJV)-The rich rules over the poor, and the borrower is servant to the lender.

Roman13:8(KJV)-Owe no one anything except to love one another, for he who loves another has fulfilled the law.

5.TIME:BE discipline with Your time if you want to prosper.

Time is a currency that must not be wasted; a wasted time is a wasted life, money, energy and destiny.

Psalm90:12(KJV)-To the end my glory may sing praise to You and not be silent. O LORD my God, I will give thanks to You forever.

Manage your time, avoid those who drain your energy and waste your time through conversation.

Ephesians5:16(KJV)- Redeeming the time, because the days are evil.

Anybody who does not respect your time don't value and respect your Assignment.

Ecclesiastes3:2(KJV)-A time to be born, and a time to die; a time to pluck what is planted;

For you to prosper you must be Discipline with your time; Don't use your time to play, work for your money.

Even in offices let people know that you are a worker.

6.YOUR THOUGHT: Discipline your thought, you can't think poor and expect to be rich.

Proverb4:23(KJV)- Keep your heart with all diligence, for out of it spring the issues of life.
The reason many are sinking is because of they are thinking poor.

Ephesians 3:20(KJV)-Now to Him who is able to do exceedingly abundantly above all that we ask or think, according to the power that works in us,

if you are praying for prosperity and you're your thinking is poverty you will end up being poor.

Philippians 4:8(KJV)-Finally, brethren, whatever things are true, whatever things are noble, whatever things are just, whatever things are pure, whatever things are lovely, whatever things are of good report, if there is any virtue and if there is anything praiseworthy—

meditate on these things.

7.YOUR WORD AND TALK: Discipline your word and talk.
Speak right for things to go right.

Proverb18:20-21(KJV)-A man's stomach shall be satisfied from the fruit of his mouth, and from the produce of his lips he shall be filled.21-Death and life are in the power of the tongue, and those who love it will eat its fruit.

Proverb 12:14(KJV)-A man will be satisfisifed with good by the fruit of his mouth, and the recompense of a man's hands will be rendered to him.

if you don't know what to talk keep quiet.

Colossians2:4(KJV)-Now this I say lest anyone should deceive you with persuasive words.

Mark11:23(KJV)-"For assuredly, I say to you, whoever says to this mountain, 'Be removed and be cast into the sea,' and does not doubt in his heart, but believes that those things he says will come to pass, he will have whatever he says.

8.TITHING: Discipline yourself in tithing; If you are not discipline you will not pay tithe.

Malachi 3:10(KJV)-Bring all the tithes into the storehouse, that there may be food in My house, and prove Me now in this ," says the LORD of hosts, "If I will not open for you the windows of heaven And pour out for you such blessing That there will not be room enough to receive it.

Tampering with your tithe is a sign of greed; it takes Discipline not to Tamper with your tithe.
Luke23:34(KJV)-Then Jesus said, "Father, forgive them, for they do not know what there are do." And they divided His garments and cast lots.

Discipline yourself so that you will tamper with your tithe, so that things will not be tight for you.

9.YOUR GIVING: Be Discipline in Your Giving.

Proverb11:24(KJV)-There is no one who scatters, yet increases more; and there is no one who withholds more than is right, but it leads to poverty.

Genesis8:22(KJV)-"While the earth remains, seedtime and harvest, and cold and heat, and winter and summer, and day and night shall not cease."

Galatians6:7,9(KJV)-Do not be deceived, God is not mocked; for whatever a man sows, that he will reap.9- And let us not grow weary while doing good, for in due season we shall reap if we do not lose heart.

Be discipline, always ensure that you give God greater than what you give to people.

2 Corinthians 6:7(KJV)-By the word of truth, by the power of God, by the armor of righteousness on the right hand and on the left,

luke23:34(KJV)-Then Jesus said , "Father, forgive them, for they do not know what they do." And they divided His garments and cast lots.

It takes Discipline to prosper and it takes discipline to give.

Ecclesiastes11:6(KJV)-In the morning sow your seed, and in the evening do not withhold your hand; for you do not know which one will prosper, either this or that, or whether both alike will be good.

1 Chronicle29:1(KJV)-Furthermore King David said to all the congregation: "My son Solomon, whom alone God has chosen, is young and inexperienced; and the work is great, because the temple is not for man but for the LORD God.

Every genuine giver is who you should give back to.

ABOUT THE AUTHOR

ENGR. Samuel Chukwubuide Stephen is a grounded Christian and engineer. He had acquired many certificates from Institute of management and Technology Enugu, Enugu state Nigeria.

He is a great writer and researcher he has published many Christian book and transform many life's through his book.